A Character Building Book ™

Learning About Determination from the Life of
Gloria Estefan

Jeanne Strazzabosco

The Rosen Publishing Group's
PowerKids Press ™
New York

Published in 1996 by The Rosen Publishing Group, Inc.
29 East 21st Street, New York, NY 10010

First Edition

Book design: Erin McKenna

Photo credits: Cover © Archive Photos; p. 7 © Mark Bolster/International Stock; p. 11 © Yves-Guy Berges/Gamma; all other photos © AP/Wide World Photos.

Strazzabosco, Jeanne.
    Learning about determination from the life of Gloria Estefan / by Jeanne M. Strazzabosco.
        p.   cm. — (A character building book)
    Includes index.
    Summary: A biography of the Cuban-born rock singer with a focus on her determination to succeed and be happy in spite of serious obstacles.
    ISBN 0-8239-2416-5
    1. Estefan, Gloria—Juvenile literature. 2. Singers—United States—Biography—Juvenile literature. 3. Determination (Personality trait)—Juvenile literature. [1. Estefan, Gloria. 2. Singers. 3. Rock music. 4. Determination (Personality trait). 5. Cuban Americans—Biography. 6. Women—Biography.] I. Title. II. Series.
ML3930.E85S77 1996
782.42164'092—dc20
[B]   96-14295
                                                                                         CIP
                                                                                          AC

Manufactured in the United States of America

Table of Contents

Determined to Succeed

Gloria María Fajardo was born in **Havana** (hah-VAN-ah), **Cuba** (KYOO-bah), in 1958. In 1959, a man named Fidel Castro became the leader of Cuba. Anyone who did not like the way Castro ran the country was in danger. Gloria's father had worked for the former leader. So he moved his family from Cuba to Miami, Florida. He returned to Cuba to fight Castro. But he was captured and put into prison.

Gloria has lived through hard times. Her **determination** (dee-ter-min-AY-shun) to succeed helped her get through these hard times.

◀ *Gloria faced many challenges in her life. But she was determined to be happy and successful. And she is.*

5

Life in Miami

Gloria's childhood was not easy. She and her mother lived alone in Miami. She did not see her father for two years. At that time, many people were **prejudiced** (PREH-juh-disd) against Cubans. Gloria and her mom finally found an apartment in a poor neighborhood. They could not afford sheets for their beds or pots to cook in. They had hardly enough money to buy food.

Gloria was scared and missed her dad. But she was determined to make her life better. She helped her mom at home and worked hard in school.

When Gloria and her mom arrived in Miami, Cubans were not welcome in areas such as Miami Beach. ▶

Learning English

Gloria had never spoken English before she moved to Miami. At home she spoke Spanish. But Gloria loved learning. She soon **excelled** (ek-SELD) in English. She also helped her mom improve her English. Only six months after starting school, Gloria won an award for reading in English. Later she learned another language, French. In high school she was a straight-A student.

◀ *Gloria's hard work in school helped her get the things she wanted in life. She even had the chance to meet the former President of the United States, George Bush.*

Dad Comes Home

After spending two years in prison, Gloria's father was set free. He moved to Miami to live with his family. Soon after, he left to fight for his new country in the Vietnam War. When Gloria was 11, her father returned from the war. He was very sick from **chemicals** (KEM-ih-kulz) that had been used in the war. Gloria's mother worked as a teacher. Gloria cared for her father and her younger sister for nearly six years.

Many soldiers who bravely fought in the Vietnam War were sick or hurt when they returned home. ▶

Gloria's Love of Music

In her free time, Gloria wrote songs, sang, and played the guitar. Gloria loved music. In high school, Gloria heard a band called the Miami Latin Boys. She met a member of the band, Emilio Estefan, Jr. He was also from Cuba. He helped Gloria and her friends put a band together to sing at a family birthday party. Gloria discovered that she loved to perform. Although she loved music, Gloria kept doing well at school. She earned a **scholarship** (SKOL-er-ship), which paid for her to go to college.

◀ *Gloria learned that she loved to sing and perform on stage.*

Singing

One day, Gloria and her family went to a wedding. The Miami Latin Boys were playing there. Emilio saw Gloria and asked if she wanted to sing a few songs with the band. She did, and everyone enjoyed her singing. A few weeks later, Emilio asked her to join the band. She agreed, but could only sing on the weekends and on holidays. She was still in college and wanted to do well in her courses.

Together, Emilio and Gloria worked hard to become famous and successful. ▶

Overcoming Shyness

When she was done with college, Gloria sang with the band full time. They changed their name to Miami Sound Machine. Gloria and Emilio fell in love and were married.

Singing was Gloria's career. She wrote many of the songs the band performed. She enjoyed being on stage, but she always stayed at the back. She was shy. But she was determined to overcome her shyness. And she did. The band became very popular. They even won the American Music Award for the Best Rock Group of the Year.

◄ *Once Gloria overcame her shyness, she became an even better performer.*

The Accident

One day, Gloria, Emilio, and their son Nayib were traveling to their next concert. All of a sudden a truck slammed into the back of their bus. Emilio and Nayib were okay. But Gloria had broken her back. She was in terrible pain.

At the hospital, doctors **operated** (OP-er-ay-tid) on her back. It was a scary time for Gloria and her family. They were afraid Gloria wouldn't be able to walk again. But the operation was successful, and Gloria was sent home.

After the accident, Gloria's family was afraid she would never walk again. But Gloria knew she could do it. ▶

Determined to Recover

Gloria was able to walk, but it was very painful. It was important to Gloria to return to the stage and sing. So she began to exercise many times a day to help her back heal properly. Each day Gloria did hundreds of sit-ups to make her back stronger. She was in great pain, but she never complained. She was determined to return to the stage and begin singing again. Within one year she was performing concerts again.

◀ *Gloria was determined to get back on stage. And she did. She gave this concert only 10 months after the accident.*

A Success Story

Today, Gloria still loves singing and is successful at writing, recording, and performing her songs. Many of her songs have become hits. She and her family live in a beautiful house in Miami overlooking the water. She and Emilio now have a baby girl, named Emily, too. Gloria has endless amounts of energy and devotion to her family and her career. She was determined to make her life better, and she did.

Glossary

chemical (KEM-ih-kul) Basic building blocks from which things are made.

Cuba (KYOO-bah) Island country about 60 miles south of the United States.

determination (dee-ter-min-AY-shun) Firmness of purpose.

excel (ek-SEL) Do very well at something.

Havana (hah-VAN-ah) Capital city of Cuba.

operate (OP-er-ayt) To perform surgery.

prejudice (PREH-juh-dis) Judging a group of people by the actions of one person.

scholarship (SKOL-er-ship) Gift of money for education.

Index